The
Practical Life Skills Workbook

Self-Assessments, Exercises & Educational Handouts

Ester A. Leutenberg
John J. Liptak, EdD

Illustrated by
Amy L. Brodsky, LISW

Whole Person Associates
Duluth, Minnesota

Whole Person
101 W. 2nd St., Suite 203
Duluth, MN 55802

800-247-6789

books@wholeperson.com
www.wholeperson.com

The Practical Life Skills Workbook
Self-Assessments, Exercises & Educational Handouts

Printed in the United States of America

10 9 8 7 6 5 4 3 2 1

Editorial Director: Carlene Sippola
Art Director: Joy Morgan Dey

Library of Congress Control Number: 2009000000
ISBN: 978-1-57025-234-1

Using This Book *(For the professional)*

Practical life skills are actually more important than a person's intelligence quotient (IQ). They are those invaluable skills people use every day that, if used effectively, allow them to create the life they desire and to access their inner resources needed to succeed.* Life skills are necessary to help people take charge and manage their personal and professional lives in an increasingly complex society. Life skills also help people manage change and deal effectively with their environments and the people in those environments. All people possess life skills that dictate their level of effectiveness in meeting the demands of everyday life.

The most important reason why life skills intelligence is more important than traditional intelligence is that, unlike the knowledge measured by traditional Intelligence Quotient (IQ) tests, life skills can be learned or refined so that you can lead a successful, satisfying and productive life.* A person's life skills IQ is comprised of many other types of intelligence including:

Physical Intelligence — focused on nutritional practices; interest in regular exercise; consistent and adequate sleep; practical and safe use of substances; optimism about one's ability to take care of health problems; and respect for one's own body.

Mental Intelligence — focused on the ability to engage in clear thinking and recall of information, with minimal interference from emotional baggage; ability to think independently and critically; possession of basic reasoning skills; open to new ideas; knowledge of one's cultural heritage; and an interest in lifelong learning.

Career Intelligence — focused on maximizing one's skills and abilities; the ability to maintain a sense of control over the occupational demands in the workplace; power to balance time and energy spent at work, with family and leisure; knowledge of one's interests, values, and personality; and knowledge of workplace politics, policies, and procedures.

Emotional Intelligence — focused on awareness of one's emotions; the ability to maintain an even emotional state with appropriate emotional responses in reaction to life events; the ability to maintain control over emotional states; the ability to experience happiness and positive emotional states; and the ability to understand one's feelings.

Social Intelligence — focused on sharing intimacy, friendship, and membership in groups; the ability to practice active listening and empathy; interest in caring for others; and open to caring and showing commitment to the common good of people, community, and the world.

Spiritual Intelligence — focused on issues of meaning, values, and purpose; interest in the importance of and search for clarity; search for greater meaning in life; commitment to faith and optimism; interest in developing the inner self and identifying purpose to life; and an ability to see the whole picture, not just isolated events.

(Continued)

---

*Liptak, J.J. (2007). *Life Skills IQ Test*. New York: Penguin Publishing.

Using This Book *(For the professional, continued)*

The Practical Life Skills Workbook contains five separate sections to help participants learn more about themselves and the competencies they possess in many life skills areas. Participants will learn about the importance of practical life skills in their daily lives. They will complete assessments and activities to make them better managers of life and to assist their development of greater life skills.

The sections of this book are:

PROBLEM-SOLVING STYLE SCALE helps individuals understand how they attempt to solve problems, and provides instruction to enhance their problem-solving ability.

MONEY MANAGEMENT STYLE SCALE helps individuals to identify their style in managing money, and provides instruction for effective money management.

TIME MANAGEMENT SKILLS SCALE helps individuals identify how effective they are at managing their time, and provides instruction for better time management.

PERSONAL CHANGE SCALE helps individuals identify the changes they are experiencing in their lives, and provides instruction for managing change.

SELF-AWARENESS SCALE helps individuals identify their level of self-awareness related to their emotions, self-confidence and self-assessment.

These sections serve as avenues for individual self-reflection, as well as for group experiences revolving around identified topics of importance. Each assessment includes directions for easy administration, scoring and interpretation. Each section includes exploratory activities, reflective journaling activities and educational handouts to help participants discover their habitual effective and ineffective life skills and provides instruction to enhance their life skills.

The art of self-reflection goes back many centuries and is rooted in many of the world's greatest spiritual and philosophical traditions. Socrates, the ancient Greek philosopher, was known to walk the streets engaging the people he met in philosophical reflection and dialogue. He felt that this type of activity was so important in life that he went so far as to proclaim, "The unexamined life is not worth living!" The unexamined life is one in which the same routine is continually repeated without ever thinking about its meaning to one's life and how this life really could be lived. However, a structured reflection and examination of beliefs, assumptions, characteristics, and patterns can provide a better understanding, which can lead to a more satisfying life. A greater level of self-understanding about important life skills is often necessary to make positive, self-directed changes in the negative patterns a person may keep repeating. The assessments and exercises in this book can help promote this self-understanding. Through involvement in the in-depth activities, the participant claims ownership in the development of positive patterns.

Using This Book *(For the professional, continued)*

Journaling is an extremely powerful tool for enhancing self-discovery, learning, transcending traditional problems, breaking ineffective life habits, and helping the person to heal from psychological traumas of the past. From a physical point of view, writing reduces stress and lowers muscle tension, blood pressure and heart rate levels. Psychologically, writing reduces sadness, depression and general anxiety, and leads to a greater level of life satisfaction and optimism. Behaviorally, writing leads to enhanced social skills, emotional intelligence and creativity. It also leads to improved writing skills which then leads to more self-confidence in the workplace.

By combining reflective assessment and journaling, participants will be exposed to a powerful method of combining verbalizing and writing to reflect on and solve problems. Participants will become more aware of the strengths and weaknesses of their daily life skills.

Preparation for using the assessments and activities in this book is important. The authors suggest that prior to administering any of the assessments in this book, you complete them yourself. This will familiarize you with the format of the assessments, the scoring directions, the interpretation guides and the journaling activities. Although the assessments are designed to be self-administered, scored and interpreted, this familiarity will help prepare facilitators to answer questions about the assessments for participants.

The Assessments, Journaling Activities and Educational Handouts

The Assessments, Journaling Activities, and Educational Handouts in *The Practical Life Skills Workbook* are reproducible and ready to be photocopied for participants' use. Assessments contained in this book focus on self-reported data and can be used by psychologists, counselors, therapists and career consultants. Accuracy and usefulness of the information provided is dependent on the truthful information that each participant provides through self-examination. By being honest, participants help themselves to learn about unproductive and ineffective patterns, and to uncover information that might be keeping them from being as happy and/or as successful as they might be.

An assessment instrument can provide participants with valuable information about themselves; however, it cannot measure or identify everything about them. The purpose of an assessment is not to pigeon-hole certain characteristics, but rather to allow participants to explore all of their characteristics. This book contains self-assessments, not tests. Tests measure knowledge or whether something is right or wrong. For the assessments in this book, there are no right or wrong answers. These assessments ask for personal opinions or attitudes about a topic of importance in the participant's career and life.

When administering assessments in this workbook, remember that the items are generically written so that they will be applicable to a wide variety of people but will not account for every possible variable for every person. Use them to help participants identify possible negative themes in their lives and find ways to break the hold that these patterns and their effects have.

Advise the participants taking the assessments that they should not spend too much time trying to analyze the content of the questions; their initial response will most likely be true. Regardless of individual scores, encourage participants to talk about their findings and their feelings pertaining to what they have discovered about themselves. Talking about health, wellness, and overall well-being can enhance the life of participants. These wellness exercises can be used by group facilitators working with any populations who want to strengthen their overall wellness.

A particular score on any assessment does not guarantee a participant's level of life skills. Use discretion when using any of the information or feedback provided in this workbook. The use of these assessments should not be substituted for consultation and/or wellness planning with a health care professional.

Thanks to the following professionals whose input in this book has been so valuable!

Carol Butler, MS Ed, RN, C

Kathy Khalsa, OTR/L

Jay Leutenberg

Kathy Liptak, Ed.D.

Eileen Regen, M.Ed., CJE

Lucy Ritzic, OTR/L

Layout of the Book

This book includes:

- **Assessment Instruments** – Self-assessment inventories with scoring directions and interpretation materials. Group facilitators can choose one or more of the activities relevant to their participants.

- **Activity Handouts** – Practical questions and activities that prompt self-reflection and promote self-understanding. These questions and activities foster introspection and promote pro-social behaviors.

- **Journaling Activities** – Self-exploration activities and journaling exercises specific to each assessment to enhance self-discovery, learning and healing.

- **Educational Handouts** – Handouts designed to enhance instruction can be used individually or in groups. They can be distributed, converted into masters for overheads or transparencies, or written down on a board and discussed.

Who should use this program?

This book has been designed as a practical tool for helping professional therapists, counselors, psychologists, teachers, group leaders, etc. Depending on the role of the professional using *The Practical Life Skills Workbook* and the specific group's needs, these sections can be used individually, combined, or implemented as part of an integrated curriculum for a more comprehensive approach.

Why use self-assessments?

Self-assessments are important in teaching various health and wellness skills. Participants will:

- Become aware of the primary motivators that guide behavior.

- Explore and learn to indentify potentially harmful situations.

- Explore the effects of messages received in childhood.

- Gain insight that will guide behavioral change.

- Focus thinking on behavioral goals for change.

- Uncover resources they possess that can help to cope with problems and difficulties.

- Explore personal characteristics without judgment.

- Develop full awareness of personal strengths and weaknesses.

Because the assessments are presented in a straightforward and easy-to-use format, individuals can self-administer, score, and interpret each assessment independently.

Introduction for the Participant

Have you ever been frustrated because you keep reliving negative events in your life? Do you feel like you are losing at the game we call life? Do you want to be living a more extraordinary and successful life? If you answered yes to any of these questions, this workbook is for you. Most of us have never learned the practical life skills we need to succeed. Because of this, many of us have had to learn our life skills in the real world through the "school of hard knocks."

We all go to school to learn the basics of math, reading, writing, and history. However, when we step out into the real world beyond school, we often find that the types of challenges and problems we encounter are very different from what we learned in school. We begin to learn that to be successful in life, we must learn more about social relationships, managing change in our lives, leading and following others, getting along with co-workers, managing money and time, and solving problems to name a few skills. These are called life skills, and some people are better at developing and using them than others. The good news is that these are skills you can learn and improve with practice.

Life skills practice allows you to develop skills needed for human development and skills that will enable you to deal effectively with the personal challenges and changes that occur in your life. Life skills, whether they are effective in helping you achieve your goals, or not, have a tendency to keep repeating themselves if they are left unexamined. That is the reason that many people go through life using ineffective life skills over and over again and expecting different results each time. Once you have identified your negative patterns and skills, you will have the power to alter them so that you begin to experience positive results as you build your repertoire of positive and strong life skills.

This book, *The Practical Life Skills Workbook*, is designed to help you learn more about yourself, identify your effective and ineffective life skills, and find better ways to use these skills to positively adapt to and deal with the unique challenges of life and career.

The Practical Life Skills Workbook
TABLE OF CONTENTS

TABLE OF CONTENTS *(continued)*

TABLE OF CONTENTS *(continued)*

SECTION I:
Problem-Solving Style Scale

Name_____

Date_____

Problem-Solving Stlye Scale Directions

Problems occur in the lives of all people. The ability to solve problems determines how satisfied we are in the many aspects of our lives. By being able to solve problems effectively, we can live a healthier and less stressful life. We may choose different approaches to solving problems. The approach that one uses is largely based on one's own personality. The Problem-Solving Style Scale is designed to help you understand how you attempt to solve problems in life and to give you additional skills in effective problem solving.

Read each of the statements and decide how descriptive the statement is of you. Circle the number of your response of each statement.

In the following example, the circled 1 indicates the statement is not at all descriptive of the person completing the inventory:

	A Lot Like Me	Somewhat Like Me	A Little Like Me	Not Like Me
When I solve a problem . . .				
I focus on what really happened to cause the problem	4	3	2	(1)

This is not a test and there are no right or wrong answers. Do not spend too much time thinking about your answers. Your initial response will likely be the most true for you. Be sure to respond to every statement.

(Turn to the next page and begin)

Problem-Solving Style Scale

	A Lot Like Me	Somewhat Like Me	A Little Like Me	Not Like Me
1. When I solve a problem . . .				
I focus on what really happened to cause the problem	4	3	2	1
I am attentive to specifics and details	4	3	2	1
I look for the immediate costs and benefits	4	3	2	1
I look for a practical solution to the problem	4	3	2	1
I look at the problem realistically	4	3	2	1
I rely on experience and standard ways to solve them	4	3	2	1
I like to gather as many facts as possible	4	3	2	1

TOTAL #1 = _____

	A Lot Like Me	Somewhat Like Me	A Little Like Me	Not Like Me
1. When I solve a problem . . .				
I try to solve the problem based on intuitive, "gut" feelings	4	3	2	1
I look at the big picture, not small details	4	3	2	1
I do what feels right	4	3	2	1
I always look for new, creative ways to solve them	4	3	2	1
I rely on internal signals about what feels good	4	3	2	1
I focus on the meaning of the problem to all involved	4	3	2	1
I value insights over facts	4	3	2	1

TOTAL #2 = _____

(Continued on the next page)

(Problem-Solving Style Scale, continued)

3. When I solve a problem . . .

	A Lot Like Me	Somewhat Like Me	A Little Like Me	Not Like Me
I look at it logically	4	3	2	1
I analyze the facts and put them in order	4	3	2	1
I want to find the one right answer	4	3	2	1
I analyze the problem objectively	4	3	2	1
I pay attention to all details of the problem	4	3	2	1
I hesitate to add emotions to the problem situation	4	3	2	1
I concentrate on the problem, not personal/group harmony	4	3	2	1

TOTAL #3 = _____

4. When I solve a problem . . .

	A Lot Like Me	Somewhat Like Me	A Little Like Me	Not Like Me
I try to please others involved in the problem situation	4	3	2	1
I think about the people involved as much as the task	4	3	2	1
I try to sense how others feel about my solutions	4	3	2	1
I want the best solution for everyone involved	4	3	2	1
I use my emotions as part of the process	4	3	2	1
I try to work out a solution in harmony with others	4	3	2	1
I do not analyze the problem in a logical way	4	3	2	1

TOTAL #4 = _____

(Go to the Scoring Directions on the next page)

Problem-Solving Style Scale
Scoring Directions

The Problem-Solving Style Scale is designed to measure your approach to solving problems that occur in your life, relationships and career. For each of the four sections, add the scores you circled for each of the items. Put that total on the line marked "Total" at the end of each section.

Then, transfer your totals to the spaces below:

1. TOTAL   =   _____ Practical Thinking

2. TOTAL   =   _____ Intuitive Reaction Thinking

3. TOTAL   =   _____ Logical Thinking

4. TOTAL   =   _____ Social Sensitive Thinking

The area in which you scored the highest tends to be your problem-solving style. Similarly, the area in which you scored the lowest tends to be your least preferred problem-solving style. Now turn to the next page for a description of each of the four scales on the assessment.

Profile Interpretation

SCALE 1 — A PRACTICAL THINKING problem-solving style is one in which you take in information that is real and tangible. You want to know what really is happening in the problem situation. You are observant about the specifics of what is going on around you and are especially attuned to the practical realities of the problem situation. You tend to notice specifics and enjoy looking at the facts. You may overlook recurring themes, focusing instead on the factual and the concrete issues involved in the problem situation. You will rely on and trust your previous experience in dealing with similar problems.

If this is your style:

> You are oriented to the present
>
> You focus on the real and actual
>
> You trust your experience from previous problem situations
>
> You trust facts rather than other people
>
> You are very observant
>
> You are able to remember specifics about the problem
>
> You understand ideas through practical applications
>
> You build carefully toward conclusions

Write about a time when the Practical Thinking problem-solving style has worked well for you.

_____

_____

_____

_____

Write about a time when the Practical Thinking problem-solving style has NOT worked well.

_____

_____

_____

_____

(Continued on the next page)

Profile Interpretation

SCALE 2 — An INTUITIVE REACTION THINKING problem-solving style is one in which you solve problems based on "gut-level" reactions. You tend to rely on your internal signals. You identify and choose a solution based on what you feel is the best possible solution for everyone involved. You do not spend a lot of time collecting facts and gathering information before you decide on a solution. This style can be useful when factual data is not available. It is important not to substitute intuition for gathering-needed information to solve the problem. You often solve problems based on hunches or your "sixth-sense" about the problem situation.

If this is your style:

You are oriented to the future

You communicate creatively

You develop imaginative solutions to problems

You reach solutions quickly, based on your hunches

You look for similarities in other problems you have needed to solve

You need the problem to make sense to you

You are attuned to seeing new possibilities

You see the big picture

Write about a time when the Intuitive Reaction Thinking problem-solving style has worked well for you.

_____

_____

_____

_____

Write a time when the Intuitive Reaction Thinking problem-solving style has NOT worked.

_____

_____

_____

_____

(Continued on the next page)

Profile Interpretation

SCALE #3 — A LOGICAL THINKING problem-solving style involves the exploration of the problem and the affects of your environment. Using this style, you identify the problem that has occurred, explore alternatives in solving the problem, and develop a plan for solving the problem based on information. You carefully weigh the costs and benefits of the various ways to solve the problem. You gather and consider additional information about alternatives and the possible consequences of each alternative. The ultimate solution you find to the problem is based on a logical problem-solving approach.

If this is your style:

You are analytical

You use cause and effect reasoning

You rely on logic

You are reasonable

You have good common-sense

You want everyone to be treated the equally

You are energized by critiquing possible solutions to problems

You like to mentally remove yourself from the situation

Write about a time when the Logical Thinking problem-solving style has worked well for you.

_____

_____

_____

_____

Write about a time when the Logical Thinking problem-solving style has NOT worked well.

_____

_____

_____

_____

(Continued on the next page)

Profile Interpretation

SCALE 4 — A SOCIAL SENSITIVE THINKING problem-solving style is one in which you want to find the best answer for all people involved (tending primarily on their emotions and values, and are most comfortable when they add emotion to the problem situation.) You will most often depend on a subjective analysis of the problem, rather than focusing on facts and figures. You try to mentally place yourself in the other person's or peoples' places so that you can identify with them. You will solve problems based on your value system that honors other people in the problem situation. You are caring and want to support everyone involved in the problem. This indicates a high level of interpersonal skills.

If this is your style:

You are empathetic to others in the situation

You are guided by your own personal issues

You are compassionate

You assess the impact of the problem on other people

You strive for harmony in resolving problems

Others call you tenderhearted

You always try to treat others fairly

You believe that positive interactions are critical in solving problems

Write about a time when the Social Sensitive Thinking problem-solving style has worked well for you.

_____

_____

_____

Write about a time when the Social Sensitive Thinking problem-solving style has NOT worked well.

_____

_____

_____

Becoming a Skilled Problem Solver

Look back at some of the problems you have solved in the past. Problems may have dealt with your relationships, education, or aspects of your job. List these problems and write down how you have approached a solution and the patterns that you notice.

Problems I Have Solved

Example of when I could have used the PRACTICAL THINKING style to solve a problem better than I solved it:

_____

_____

_____

Example of when I could have used the INTUITIVE REACTION THINKING style to solve a problem better than I solved it:

_____

_____

_____

Example of when I could have used the LOGICAL THINKING style to solve a problem better than I solved it:

_____

_____

_____

Example of when I could have used the SOCIAL SENSITIVE THINKING style to solve a problem better than I solved it:

_____

_____

_____

The Problem-Solving Process Outline *(1)*

There is no simple step-by-step process that will guarantee you a solution to every problem you encounter in your life. The problem-solving process is a search for, and implementation of, the best possible solution for a specific problem. As a problem solver, you will develop your own method for solving problems. One of the best methods for doing this is to try to use the most effective aspects of the four different styles. The following is an outline of how to integrate the four styles in the problem-solving process.

What is a problem that you have had in the past or one that you are presently struggling with?

Step 1 — Define the problem by using **Practical Thinking** characteristics to see the problem situation as it really is. You can do so by answering some of the following questions:

What can you see that is causing the problem?

Where is it occurring?

How is it occurring?

When is it occurring?

With whom is it occurring?

Why is it occurring?

What is your role in the problem?

What has already been tried to resolve the situation?

Step 2 — Consider the possibilities using **Intuitive Reaction Thinking** characteristics to brainstorm all possible solutions to the problem. You can do so by answering some of the following questions:

What other ways can you look at the problem?

What does the information that you have gathered suggest to you?

What are the connections to the bigger picture?

How do the other people fit into this picture?

What do you think is causing the problem?

What are some possible ways to approach the problem?

(Continued on the next page)

The Problem-Solving Process Outline (2)

Step 3 — Weigh the consequences of courses of action to resolve the problem using **Logical Thinking** characteristics. You can do so by answering some of the following questions:

What are the pros of each option?

What are the cons of each option?

What are the logical consequences of each option?

How does each option apply equally to each person involved?

Step 4 — Weigh the alternatives to each course of action using **Social Sensitive Thinking** characteristics. You can do so by answering some of the following questions:

How does each alternative fit with my values?

How will the other people involved in the situation be affected?

How will each alternative contribute to harmony for all people involved?

How will each alternative enhance positive interactions?

Step 5 — Decide which aspects of Steps 1 – 4 will be most effective in solving this problem.

Step 6 — Act on your decision.

Step 7 — Evaluate whether the problem has been resolved or not

Complete the following four Problem Solving activity pages.

Problem-Solving Activity *(1)*

Identify a major problem you are facing.

_____

Complete this 4-page activity that will help you learn and apply the problem-solving process:

Step 1 — Define the problem by using PRACTICAL THINKING characteristics to see the problem situation as it really is. You can do so by answering some of the following questions:

What can you see that is causing the problem?

_____

Where is it occurring?

_____

How is it occurring?

_____

When is it occurring?

_____

With whom is it occurring?

_____

Why is it occurring?

_____

_____

What is your role in the problem?

_____

_____

What has already been tried to resolve the situation?

_____

_____

Problem-Solving Activity (2)

Step 2 — Consider the possibilities using INTUITIVE REACTION characteristics to brainstorm all possible solutions to the problem. You can do so by asking some of the following questions:

What other ways can we look at the problem?

_____

_____

What does the information that you have gathered suggest to you?

_____

_____

What are the connections to the bigger picture?

_____

_____

How do the other people fit into this picture?

_____

_____

What do you think is causing the problem?

_____

_____

What are some possible ways to approach the problem?

_____

_____

Problem-Solving Activity *(3)*

Step 3 — Weigh the consequences of courses of action to resolve the problem using LOGICAL THINKING characteristics. You can do so by asking some of the following questions:

What are the pros of each option?

_____

_____

_____

_____

What are the cons of each option?

_____

_____

_____

_____

What are the logical consequences of each option?

_____

_____

_____

_____

How does each option apply equally to each person involved?

_____

_____

_____

_____

_____

Problem-Solving Activity *(4)*

Step 4 — Weigh the alternatives to each course of action using SOCIAL SENSITIVE THINKING characteristics. You can do so by asking some of the following questions:

How does each alternative fit with my values?

_____

_____

How will the other people involved in the situation be affected?

_____

_____

How will each alternative contribute to harmony for all people involved?

_____

_____

How will each alternative enhance positive interactions?

_____

_____

Step 5 – Decide which aspects of Steps 1 – 4 will be most effective in solving this problem.

_____

Step 6 – Make a final decision:

_____

Step 7 – Act on your decision. What do you need to do to implement your decision?

_____

_____

Step 8 – How did the problem get resolved?

_____

_____

My Problems

What types of problems do you encounter the most? (conflicts with relatives, communications, etc.)

_____

_____

_____

_____

_____

_____

_____

_____

What areas of your life are most affected?

_____

_____

_____

_____

_____

_____

_____

_____

Problem-Solving

With whom do you mostly have problems?

_____

_____

_____

_____

_____

_____

_____

_____

What aspects of the other problem-solving styles do you want to integrate into your style?

_____

_____

_____

_____

_____

_____

_____

_____

Logical Thinking Method

This technique includes clarifying the problem, analyzing major causes of the problem, identifying alternatives, assessing them, choosing and implementing an option, and evaluating the outcome.

Divide:
Break problems into smaller, solvable problems

Brainstorm:
List all of the possible solutions, no matter how outrageous they seem

Test:
Pose possible solutions to the problem and then try to prove the accuracy of the solutions. Suggest how each might work.

Research:
Get valid information from trusted people and respected publications.

Past Experience:
Remember similar problems, how you solved them and what worked. Ask others what worked for them.

Trial-and-error:
Create and implement solutions, then see if they work

Incubation / Wait:
Stop focusing on the problem, and allow the subconscious to work so that the solution will "pop out" while you work on other things

Characteristics That Make Solving a Problem Difficult

- Not knowing all of the facts before trying to solve the problem

- Multiple possible outcomes

- Multiple views of others

- Large numbers of items and decisions to be made to solve a major problem

- Time is of the essense

*Adapted from J. Funke (1995). Complex problem solving in personnel selection and training. In P.A. Frensch & J Funke (Eds), *Complex problem solving: The European Perspective.* Hillsdale, NJ: Lawrence Erlbaum Associates.

SECTION II:
Money Management Style Scale

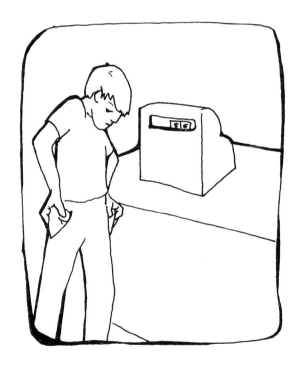

Name_____

Date_____

Money Management Stlye Scale Directions

Money management skills are difficult life skills to acquire and utilize effectively. Everyone has different styles when it comes to managing money. This scale will help you identify your money management style and skills, and learn techniques for more effective money management. The scale contains 50 statements. Read each of the statements and decide to what extent the statement describes you. For each of the statements listed, circle the number of your response on the line to the right of each statement.

In the following example, the circled 2 indicates that the statement is a little like the person taking the assessment:

	A Lot Like Me	A Little Like Me	Not Like Me
STYLE 1:			
I buy whatever brings me pleasure	3	(2)	1

This is not a test and there are no right or wrong answers. Do not spend too much time thinking about your answers. Your initial response will likely be the most true for you. Be sure to respond to every statement.

(Turn to the next page and begin)

Money Management Style Scale

	A Lot Like Me	A Little Like Me	Not Like Me
STYLE 1			
I buy whatever brings me pleasure	3	2	1
I often buy gifts for other people	3	2	1
I have a hard time budgeting my money	3	2	1
It is difficult for me to save money	3	2	1
I buy things on impulse	3	2	1
I often overspend the money I earn	3	2	1
I am often in debt	3	2	1
I am not afraid to spend all the money I have	3	2	1
No gift is priced too high for me	3	2	1
I get a thrill from buying things	3	2	1

TOTAL = _____

	A Lot Like Me	A Little Like Me	Not Like Me
STYLE 2			
I like to hold onto my money	3	2	1
I am great at saving money	3	2	1
I have a budget that I stick to	3	2	1
I will not buy non-essential items	3	2	1
I only buy what I need	3	2	1
I am focused on financial stability	3	2	1
I like the security of having money in the bank	3	2	1
I usually pay cash for my purchases	3	2	1
I am rarely in credit-card debt	3	2	1
I save at least 10 percent of my salary monthly	3	2	1

TOTAL = _____

(Continued on the next page)

(Money Management Style Scale, continued)

	A Lot Like Me	A Little Like Me	Not Like Me
STYLE 3			
I often worry about my finances	3	2	1
I feel like it is up to me to control my money	3	2	1
I check my financial account balances often	3	2	1
I often think about what might happen to my money	3	2	1
If I just had more money I could stop worrying about it	3	2	1
I worry that I will not have enough retirement savings	3	2	1
I like my money in safe investments	3	2	1
I like to be able to put my hands on my money easily	3	2	1
I worry when I make a major purchase	3	2	1
I spend a lot of emotional energy worrying about finances	3	2	1

TOTAL = _____

	A Lot Like Me	A Little Like Me	Not Like Me
STYLE 4			
I want to achieve great wealth	3	2	1
I believe that with wealth comes power and status	3	2	1
I put a lot of time into managing my money	3	2	1
I often spend hours hunting for the best investments	3	2	1
I use a personal finance computer program	3	2	1
I like to occasionally flaunt my wealth	3	2	1
I think that having a lot of money impresses people	3	2	1
I get obsessed with tracking my money	3	2	1
My self-worth comes from my investment portfolio	3	2	1
I often shift investments to earn the best returns	3	2	1

TOTAL = _____

(Continued on the next page)

(Money Management Style Scale, continued)

	A Lot Like Me	A Little Like Me	Not Like Me
STYLE 5			
I enjoy taking risks with money	3	2	1
I am competitive when it comes to money	3	2	1
I get a rush from any intense experience	3	2	1
I try to make a lot of money by playing the lottery	3	2	1
I thrive on uncertainty	3	2	1
I always go for broke with my money	3	2	1
I like the adrenaline rush from risking my money	3	2	1
Others say I am too aggressive in my investments	3	2	1
If I lose money, I believe more will come my way	3	2	1
I am motivated by variety and change	3	2	1

TOTAL = _____

(Go to the Profile Interpretation on the next page)

© 2009 WHOLE PERSON ASSOCIATES, 101 W. 2ND ST., SUITE 203, DULUTH MN 55802 ▪ 800-247-6789

Money Management Style Scale
Scoring Directions

The assessment you just completed is designed to measure your money management style. Add the numbers you've circled for each of the five sections on the previous pages. Put that total on the line marked TOTAL at the end of each section.

Transfer your totals for each of the five sections to the lines below:

Style 1: Spenders Total = _____

Style 2: Savers Total = _____

Style 3: Conscientious Managers Total = _____

Style 4: Amassers Total = _____

Style 5: Risk Takers Total = _____

Profile Interpretation

The area in which you scored the highest tends to be your money management style. Similarly, the area in which you scored the lowest tends to be your least preferred style for managing your money. Go to the section which describes your preferred money management style. If time permits, read about the other money management styles. If you had similar scores for several of the styles, read each of them and decide which money management style fits you most, or how you combine the two styles in managing your money.

For each of the styles, place a check in the box by the characteristics that sound like you.

STYLE 1: SPENDERS

As a Spender, you tend to get carried away by instant gratification in your life. You often feel compelled to spend or charge money very easily and quickly, even if you can't afford the purchases. You will shop and spend compulsively. You often find it difficult to think about doing anything else other than shopping. Shopping provides you with psychological comfort and distraction. You tend to buy things you do not even need, but it is the act of shopping and spending money that satisfies your psychological cravings. You tend to have many credit cards and many of them are probably charged to their limit. You probably feel like your debts are out of control, but find it difficult to stop the psychological "high" you get from shopping and spending money.

Characteristics:
- [ ] You frequently receive overdue notices for bills past due.
- [ ] You overspend to feel better about yourself.
- [ ] Shopping is a form of addiction for you.
- [ ] You often justify, especially to yourself, continuous buying.
- [ ] You feel like you will be happier if you purchase material things.
- [ ] You pay large amounts of money in interest on your credit cards.

(Continued on the next page)

Profile Interpretation *(Continued)*

STYLE 2: SAVERS

As a Saver, you tend to be very financially stable. You feel a sense of pride in how you have earned and now manage your money. You focus primarily on feeling safe and secure, and doing what you need to do to stay that way. Your debts tend to be under control and all of the choices you make are designed to keep you secure. You frequently check your total assets so that you will feel more psychologically and economically secure.

Characteristics:

☐ When it comes to money you are organized and focused on stability.

☐ You tend to be educated about money and financial planning strategies.

☐ You have conservative spending habits.

☐ You save to ensure the future in anticipation of possible changes in your life.

☐ You believe that the way to financial security is through steady, conservative investments.

☐ Regardless of your age, you enjoy planning for your retirement.

STYLE 3: CONSCIENTIOUS MANAGER

As a Conscientious Manager, you tend to believe that the only way to feel financially secure is to hang on to every penny you earn. You tend to continually worry about money, and often let your anxiety get in the way of having fun. You may even feel like a financial disaster is inevitable, and you want to be ready. You prefer thrift over spending, are frugal, and do without things you want. You are terribly afraid of losing your money and you want to be prepared for long periods of unemployment or for financial disaster.

Characteristics:

☐ You build a stash of money that you can fall back on in case of an emergency.

☐ You like living on a budget.

☐ You like using coupons to save money when you shop.

☐ You are disciplined about money and are interested in advertisements and sales of necessary products.

☐ You live well within your monetary means.

☐ You keep a balanced checkbook.

(Continued on the next page)

Profile Interpretation *(Continued)*

STYLE 4: AMASSERS

As an Amasser, money is about status and living as if you make more money than you really do. It is through money than you are able to keep score and compare yourself with others. You like to keep up with, and perhaps surpass, the "Joneses." You feel like the more you have, the more successful you are. Therefore, your worth is tied to your possessions. Buying upscale materials and goods provides you with psychological comfort. You may purchase nice cars, homes, and clothes but you probably do not have an emergency fund set aside for a rainy day. You may not even realize how much money you are spending, as opposed to saving or investing.

Characteristics:

☐ You probably have the drive and energy to make a lot of money.

☐ You are willing to work hard and you take great pride in your accomplishments.

☐ You are a natural achiever and enjoy spending money as a symbol of your achievements.

☐ You think that appearances are important, and you usually have high quality possessions and travel.

☐ You tend to overestimate how much you earn and underestimate how much you spend.

☐ When you see things you want, you go ahead and buy them regardless of how much they cost.

STYLE 5: RISK TAKERS

As a Risk Taker, you tend to get an exhilarating emotional rush from spending and managing money. You believe that the only way to have what you want in life is to take significant risks. You always want whatever is bigger and better in your life and your career. You like to gamble on hunches when it comes to money. You trust your instincts that your risks will pay off. You are a gambler with your money.

Characteristics:

☐ You always go for broke with your money.

☐ You tend to be charismatic and creative in earning and spending money.

☐ You don't mind unpredictability and uncertainty when it comes to managing your money.

☐ You will gamble on your own ability to make a lot of money.

☐ If you do invest your money, it will be in extremely high-risk endeavors.

☐ You like to take chances.

How You Spend Your Money

This activity is designed to help you determine the approximate amount of money you are currently spending on a monthly basis:

MONTHLY NECESSITIES

I. Home (rent, mortgage, insurance, gas, electricity, water, sewage, taxes, television, Internet access, telephone, other)

_____

_____

_____

_____

_____

II. Car (car payment, car repairs, insurance, parking, gas, other)

_____

_____

_____

_____

_____

III. Personal Needs (clothes, food, entertainment, medical, newspaper, insurance, cell phone, other)

_____

_____

_____

_____

_____

(Continued on the next page)

How You Spend Your Money *(Continued)*

MONTHLY NECESSITIES *(continued)*

IV. Children's Needs (medical/dental, education, clothes, food, child care, other)

_____

_____

_____

_____

_____

V. Financial Considerations (credit card payments, life insurance, loan repayment, taxes, other)

_____

_____

_____

_____

_____

VI. Other

_____

_____

_____

_____

_____

_____

_____

(Continued on the next page)

How You Spend Your Money

MONTHLY LUXURIES

This exercise is designed to help you separate necessities from luxuries in your life. Complete the sections below by listing your monthly luxuries in the right hand column. What themes do you see?

	LUXURIES
Home	*Satellite dish, grass-cutting service, etc.*
Car	
Personal	
Children's Needs	
Other	

Spending Habits

How are your money spending and saving habits similar or different from those of your parents?

_____

_____

_____

How did your parents money management affect you (positively or negatively)?

_____

_____

_____

If you overspend, how do you attempt to hide your tendency to overspend?

_____

_____

_____

How often do you break your budget by spending more than you make? How can you fix this situation?

_____

_____

_____

In what ways do your spending and saving habit ever cause conflict between you and significant others?

_____

_____

_____

(Continued on the next page)

Spending Habits *(Continued)*

What risk would you like to take with your money that you have been afraid to in the past?

_____

_____

What risks would you like to stop taking?

_____

_____

What is your greatest fear related to spending and saving money? Why do you have this fear?

_____

_____

_____

What feelings do you experience when spending money?

_____

_____

_____

What types of activities could you engage in to get the same pleasure you get from spending money?

_____

_____

_____

If your life, or the life of your family, has suffered because you spend money on things you cannot afford or do not spend money on things you can afford, write about it.

_____

_____

_____

My Money History

It is often helpful to look at how money was handled in your family when you were growing up:

In what town(s), state (s), and/or country(s) did you grow up?

_____

_____

_____

_____

_____

How did the location of where you grew up affect your family's money management style?

_____

_____

_____

_____

_____

How financially comfortable was your family and how has this affected your current thoughts about money?

_____

_____

_____

_____

_____

(Continued on the next page)

My Money History *(Continued)*

What were your father / male caregiver's thoughts about money and money management?

_____

_____

_____

_____

What were your mother / female caregiver's thoughts about money and money management?

_____

_____

_____

_____

How was money handled in your family?

_____

_____

_____

_____

_____

What did you learn from your parents / caregivers about money management?

_____

_____

_____

_____

_____

(Continued on the next page)

My Money History *(Continued)*

Who took care of the money management process as you were growing up?

_____

_____

_____

_____

_____

Who takes care of money management in your current family?

_____

_____

_____

_____

_____

_____

How can you manage your money more effectively in the future?

_____

_____

_____

_____

_____

_____

_____

Current Spending Behavior

Write a summary of your current spending behaviors and money management style.

_____

_____

_____

_____

_____

_____

_____

_____

_____

Write a summary of the current spending behavior of the person or people with whom you live.

_____

_____

_____

_____

_____

_____

_____

_____

_____

_____

© 2009 WHOLE PERSON ASSOCIATES, 101 W. 2ND ST., SUITE 203, DULUTH MN 55802 ▪ 800-247-6789

New Spending Behaviors

How would you like to change your spending behaviors?

_____

_____

_____

_____

_____

_____

_____

_____

How do you wish the person or people with whom you live would change their spending behaviors?

_____

_____

_____

_____

_____

_____

_____

_____

_____

Ways to Prevent Shopping Binges

- Pay with cash, check or debit cards

- Make a shopping list and stick to it

- Destroy all credit cards except for one "emergency" card

- Pay the total balance each month, IF you use a credit card

- Avoid watching television shopping channels

- Find an inexpensive hobby to rely on when the urge to spend occurs

- Avoid shopping when you feel anxious, angry or depressed

- Find healthy ways to meet your need to spend

Spending Related Behaviors

- Engaging in arguments with others about spending money

- Buying on credit and monthly payments

- Thinking obsessively about money

- Spending money thoughtlessly

- Lying about how much you spend

- Juggling bills to accommodate spending

- Refusing to purchase necessities

- Feeling euphoria when you are spending money

- Being too generous or not generous at all

SECTION III:
Time Management Skills Scale

Name_____

Date_____

Time Management Skills Scale Directions

For people who are good managers of time, time brings relaxation, satisfaction, and success. Good time managers tend to have productive work habits, effective relationships, and a successful life. For others who are managed by time opposed to being time-managers, time brings anxiety, stress, exhaustion and complication. One of the leading causes of stress is that people have too much to do and not enough time to do it. In this fast-paced society, learning how to manage your time can help you to alleviate stress and reduce anxiety in your life.

If you are struggling with time management, don't worry – you're not alone. Many people feel that there is not enough time in the day and that they need to learn effective time management skills. By learning better time management skills, you can regain control over your life. Rather than getting bogged down and not getting enough done, effective time management helps you to choose what you need to work on and when to work on it.

This assessment contains 32 statements that are related to your time management skills. Read each of the statements and decide whether or not the statement describes you. If the statement does describe you, circle the number in the YES column next to that item. If the statement does not describe you, circle the number in the NO column next to that item.

In the following example, the circled number under "Yes" indicates the statement is descriptive of the person completing the inventory.

	YES	NO
1. I have my short-term goals written down	(2)	1

This is not a test and there are no right or wrong answers. Do not spend too much time thinking about your answers. Your initial response will likely be the most true for you. Be sure to respond to every statement.

(Turn to the next page and begin)

Time Management Skills Scale

	YES	NO
GOAL SETTING		
1. I have my short-term goals written down	2	1
2. I rarely write down my plans for the future	1	2
3. I use goal setting to decide what to work on	2	1
4. I stress out about deadlines	1	2
5. I say "yes" and then regret it	1	2
6. Before I take on a task, I make sure the results are worth the time	2	1
7. I often set and work toward unattainable goals	1	2
8. I take on more commitments than I have time to complete	1	2

TOTAL = _____

	YES	NO
PRIORITIZING		
9. I hang on to mail and emails even though I know they are unimportant	1	2
10. I work on tasks starting with those I decide have the highest priority	2	1
11. I know how much time I spend on the tasks I do	2	1
12. I analyze new tasks for their importance and then prioritize them	2	1
13. I keep a prioritized "to do" list	2	1
14. I talk to my spouse/partner/boss about the priorities of tasks I am given	2	1
15. I hate to delegate jobs even though I know I cannot complete them	1	2
16. I work on projects that will yield the best results	2	1

TOTAL = _____

(Continued on the next page)

(Time Management Skills Scale, continued)

	YES	NO
PROCRASTINATING		
17. I complete most projects at the last minute	1	2
18. I put off tasks that may be too difficult	1	2
19. I often put things off because I am afraid of making mistakes	1	2
20. I have trouble meeting deadlines set for me	1	2
21. I take pride in the fact that I usually complete tasks at the last minute	1	2
22. I try to return phone calls and e-mails within 24 hours	2	1
23. I rarely have to ask for more time to complete a task	2	1
24. I must often take work home to get it done	1	2

TOTAL = _____

	YES	NO
SCHEDULING		
25. People say that I "have no sense of time"	1	2
26. I have a daily planner I carry with me	2	1
27. I have a filing system for personal papers	2	1
28. I set time aside to plan my work	2	1
29. I check my 'to-do' list regularly for new tasks	2	1
30. I have time built into my schedule to deal with unexpected events	2	1
31. I feel lost without a watch	2	1
32. I am often late	1	2

TOTAL = _____

Time Management Skills Scale
Scoring Directions

Add your scores for each of the four sections and write those numbers in the TOTAL blanks at the end of each section. Then transfer the numbers to each of the blank spaces below.

GOAL SETTING   =   _____

PRIORITIZING   =   _____

PROCRASTINATING =   _____

SCHEDULING   =   _____

Profile Interpretation

Individual Scale Scores	Result	Indications
Scores from 14 to 16	high	You tend to have very effective time management skills in this area.
Scores from 11 to 13	Moderate	You tend to have some effective time management skills, but there is room for you to improve as a manager of time.
Scores from 8 to 10	Low	You tend to have limited time management skills in this area. You need to do as much as possible to enhance your time management skills for personal and professional growth.

Read the following descriptions in the Profile Interpretations and complete the exercises that are included. Regardless of how you scored on each of the scales, you will benefit from these time-management exercises.

(Profile Interpretation continued on the next page)

Time Management Skills Scale
Profile Interpretation *(Continued)*

GOAL SETTING

People scoring low on this scale are not setting adequate goals. Once you have set goals, you can then know where you are going and what needs to be done to get there. With effective goal setting, you tend to spend your time on conflicting priorities. By setting goals, you will save yourself time, effort and frustration in the future. You need to begin setting concrete attainable goals on how you use your time.

PRIORITIZING

People scoring low on this scale need to work on prioritizing what needs to be done. Prioritizing helps you to work on those projects that are most critical. You need to develop a system for prioritizing and adding structure to your work. To work effectively, you need to work on the tasks that have the highest value and importance.

PROCRASTINATING

People scoring low on this scale need to work on getting tasks done on time and not wait until the last minute. You need to develop the habit of not procrastinating or else tasks will back up until you are unable to complete them all. You might feel like you will put things off until you are rested or that you work best when under pressure. Pressure from undone tasks can cause stress in your life that is avoidable.

SCHEDULING

People scoring low on this scale do not effectively schedule their own time. You need to begin creating a schedule that can help to keep you on track and protect you from procrastination and the stress that goes with it. Develop an awareness of the factors that may be interfering with your ability to complete your work. Scheduling will ensure that you work on priority tasks and allow for unexpected events and interruptions.

Time Management Exercises & Activities

GOAL-SETTING: Step 1 — Define Your Goals

It is important for you to determine what you would like to see happen in the future. This will help to give order and context to your daily schedule. This might include such things as being more efficient at work, getting involved with more community activities, or spending more quality time with your family. These types of goals will provide you with direction and priorities. You will need to give time and energy to the goals you develop for yourself.

The first step in setting and reaching effective goals is to define them so they are realistic and achievable. Take a look at some sample goals:

"Be successful"

"Make a lot of money"

"Be happier in my marriage"

"Be a good leader"

"Be a better parent"

Notice that these goals are vague and difficult to measure. When you are developing goals for enhanced time management, remember that the goals should have the following characteristics: they need to be Specific, Measurable, Attainable, Relevant to you, and tied to a Timeline (SMART for short). Let's take a look at each of these characteristics in more detail:

Specific: Goals must be stated in concrete, behavioral terms. For example, "I would like to travel to Quebec next summer" would be a concrete, behavioral goal.

Measurable: Goals must be measurable so that you can track your progress. For example, traveling to Quebec next summer can be measured, while "Travel more" is hard to measure.

Attainable: Goals must be within your reach or you will not be motivated to work toward them. You must feel like you have a realistic opportunity to achieve your goals. For example, feeling like you have the time, finances, and resources to travel to Europe next summer may not be realistic whereas traveling to Quebec may be a viable option.

Relevant: Goals must be important to you. For example, knowing that traveling to Quebec will allow you and your children to experience a different culture makes this goal very relevant to you.

Timed: Goals must have deadlines attached to them if they are going to motivate you, though you need to be reasonable and set deadlines that you can realistically commit to. For example, by stating that you would like to travel next summer puts a time frame on the goal you have set.

(Continued on the next page)

GOAL-SETTING: Step 1 — Define Your Goals *(Continued)*

Define your own goals. They should be positively stated and realistic, identify specific behaviors, and within your ability to achieve. Use the space below to set four or more goals in each of the following areas of your life that will help you live better.

My Personal Goals

_____

_____

_____

_____

_____

My Family / Significant Other Goals

_____

_____

_____

_____

_____

My Career / Job Goals

_____

_____

_____

_____

_____

GOAL-SETTING: Step 2 — Prioritize Your Goals

The next step is to prioritize your goals into long-term and short-term by importance. Short-term goals are objectives that you would like to achieve in a year or less. These goals may be changed or revised as new options present themselves. Long-term goals are objectives that you want to achieve over a longer period of time, and can be set five to ten years into the future. Try to clarify what is urgent, what is somewhat important, and what can wait.

Use the space below to prioritize your goals into long-range and short-range goals. Be sure to place the short-term goals first. These may be related to your personal life, your family life, or your career.

Short-Term Goals

_____

_____

_____

_____

_____

Long-Term Goals

_____

_____

_____

_____

_____

GOAL-SETTING: Step 3 — Don't Procrastinate

Procrastination is the thief of time. Procrastination means that you put off things that you need to do or want to do until a later time. You may have trouble starting to work on your goals, or you may have trouble finishing a goal because you get distracted or begin working on another goal.

Answer the following questions to help you identify what you procrastinate about:

1. Think about something you have always wanted to do, but have put off. What is it?

_____

_____

_____

2. What is keeping you from doing it?

_____

_____

_____

3. What are you avoiding?

_____

_____

_____

4. Answer the question, "What is the worst thing that could happen if I do it?"

_____

_____

_____

5. Identify a time when you can start to work on this goal:

   Day of the week:_____   Time:_____

6. When will you achieve this goal?

_____

(Continued on the next page)

GOAL-SETTING: Step 3 — Don't Procrastinate *(Continued)*

Use the worksheet below to identify other ways that you are procrastinating in reaching your goals:

REASONS I PROCRASTINATE	LUXURIES
I'm a perfectionist	
I might make a mistake	
I'm worried about a confrontation	
I have feelings of being overwhelmed	
(Write your own reason here)	

© 2009 WHOLE PERSON ASSOCIATES, 101 W. 2ND ST., SUITE 203, DULUTH MN 55802 ▪ 800-247-6789

GOAL-SETTING: Step 4 — Schedule Your Time

Scheduling is the process of allocating time for prioritized goals. It is planning time to accomplish individual goals. Strive to provide a set time schedule to achieve goals rather than having it imposed by people or conditions outside of you. For example, if your supervisor gives you an assignment on Monday to read and research something (and she needs it by Friday), set an internal deadline of Thursday to finish the assignment.

Scheduling Techniques:

1. Time Blocking — Time Blocking is setting aside (or blocking out) several hours each day to spend toward accomplishing one of your goals. When would you like to block out time for during your day?

_____

_____

_____

_____

_____

2. Break large tasks into smaller (easier to accomplish) goals. What large goal do you have that you would like to break down into smaller goals?

_____

_____

_____

_____

... And how might this plan look?

_____

_____

_____

_____

Other Time Management Techniques

To-Do Lists

To-do lists are lists of tasks that need to be completed. This tool can help you to remember tasks and not trust them to your memory alone. In this activity, you develop a list of tasks to be accomplished and when they need to be accomplished. As you complete items on the task list, you can simply check them off the list. Below, create a list of tasks you need to complete for a project at home or at work:

TASK TO DO	WHEN I NEED TO COMPLETE THE TASK	DONE
Paint the Bedroom	A week from Tuesday	✓

Protect Your Time

What are some things that you can start doing to protect your time better? Protecting your time is critical in being a good time manager. Some ways of protecting your time might include closing a door, putting a sign up and not answering your telephone.

What types of things will you do to protect your time? Complete your answers below:

PART OF MY LIFE	WHAT I WILL DO
Personal time	*(ex. Limit my computer time)*
Time with Family / Friends / and Significant Others	*(ex. Time spent with special people only)*
Time at Work	*(ex. Fewer coffee breaks)*

Be More Assertive

Be assertive when you need to be. Time is a valuable commodity. Remember that it is your time and does not belong to other people. You may need to be more assertive in protecting the time you need and not allow people to "steal" time away from you. List the people who "steal" time from you and how they do this:

PEOPLE WHO 'STEAL' TIME FROM ME	HOW THEY DO IT
Friend, Janet	She tries to 'give me the guilts' when I don't call every day.

Manage Perfectionistic Behaviors

Perfectionism is the notion that you must complete each task perfectly.

What makes you think you are a perfectionist?

_____

_____

_____

_____

_____

If so, in what areas of your life are you a perfectionist?

_____

_____

_____

_____

_____

How does that perfectionism take away your time?

_____

_____

_____

_____

_____

_____

Delegate

When you think about it, there will always be more to do than time to do it in. What types of activities do you do (ones that steal a lot of your time), that you could delegate to others? List the tasks/activities below, and the person or people to whom you could delegate these tasks/activities:

ACTIVITIES	DELEGATE TO
Personal Life	
Family Life	
Career Life	

Maintain Balance in Life

When tasks become stressful, it is usually because you are experiencing an imbalance among the various roles in your life. Think about the amount of time you spend on your personal self, your family self, your career self and your relationships. It is important for you to develop an awareness of what is most important in your life. Identify below how much time you are spending on various aspects of life. Choose from the activities listed below or feel free to write your own. In this chart, identify how you are spending your time on a daily basis. List the activities on the chart and the amount of time you spend on a typical day on that activity.

(Examples: Exercise, Work, Intimacy, Play / Leisure, Friendship, Hobbies, Community activities, Solitude and contemplation, Simple pleasures, Household chores, Eating, Caring for children, Caring for elderly parents, Commuting to work, Playing sports, Playing / Caring for animals, Educational activities, Reading, Sleeping, Family activities, Others)

24 – HOUR TIME FRAME ACTIVITIES	
7:00 am – 8:00 am	7:00 pm – 8:00 pm
8:00 am – 9:00 am	8:00 pm – 9:00 pm
9:00 am – 10:00 am	9:00 pm – 10:00 pm
10:00 am – 11:00 am	10:00 pm – 11:00 pm
11:00 am – Noon	11:00 pm – Midnight
Noon – 1:00 pm	Midnight – 1:00 am
1:00 pm – 2:00 pm	1:00 am – 2:00 am
2:00 pm – 3:00 pm	2:00 am – 3:00 am
3:00 pm – 4:00 pm	3:00 am – 4:00 am
4:00 pm – 5:00 pm	4:00 am – 5:00 am
5:00 pm – 6:00 pm	5:00 am – 6:00 am
6:00 pm – 7:00 pm	6:00 am – 7:00 am

(Continued on the next page)

Maintain Balance in Life *(Continued)*

Think again about the amount of time *you would like to spend* on your personal self, your family self, your career self and your relationships. Identify below how much time you would like to spend on various life aspects. Choose from the activities below or feel free to write your own. In this second chart, identify how you would prefer to spend your time on a daily basis. List the activities on the chart and the amount of time you would like to spend on a typical day on that activity. When you are finished, it should total 24 hours.

(Examples: Exercise, Work, Intimacy, Play / Leisure, Friendship, Hobbies, Community activities, Solitude and contemplation, Simple pleasures, Household chores, Eating, Caring for children, Caring for elderly parents, Commuting to work, Playing sports, Playing / Caring for animals, Educational activities, Reading, Sleeping, Family activities, Others)

24 – HOUR TIME FRAME ACTIVITIES	
7:00 am – 8:00 am	7:00 pm – 8:00 pm
8:00 am – 9:00 am	8:00 pm – 9:00 pm
9:00 am – 10:00 am	9:00 pm – 10:00 pm
10:00 am – 11:00 am	10:00 pm – 11:00 pm
11:00 am – Noon	11:00 pm – Midnight
Noon – 1:00 pm	Midnight – 1:00 am
1:00 pm – 2:00 pm	1:00 am – 2:00 am
2:00 pm – 3:00 pm	2:00 am – 3:00 am
3:00 pm – 4:00 pm	3:00 am – 4:00 am
4:00 pm – 5:00 pm	4:00 am – 5:00 am
5:00 pm – 6:00 pm	5:00 am – 6:00 am
6:00 pm – 7:00 pm	6:00 am – 7:00 am

Time Management Background

What was the time management like in your home when you were growing up?

_____

_____

_____

_____

_____

_____

_____

_____

_____

_____

How has that background affected your sense of time?

_____

_____

_____

_____

_____

_____

_____

_____

_____

_____

My Time Management

In what areas of your life do you already manage time well?

_____

_____

_____

_____

_____

_____

_____

_____

In what areas of your life do you want to improve time management?

_____

_____

_____

_____

_____

_____

_____

_____

_____

Benefits of Effective Time Management

By utilizing time management techniques, you will be able to:

- Improve your productivity

- Make time for things you value

- Find greater balance

- Find greater life satisfaction

- Set and achieve long and short-term goals

- Accomplish tasks and reach goals with less stress and anxiety

- Focus your energy on important tasks

Symptoms of Poor Time Management

- Forgetfulness

- Concentration

- Fatigued

- Overwhelmed

- Sleeplessness

- Irritability

- Headaches

- Worry

- Depression

SECTION IV:
Self-Awareness Scale

Name_____

Date_____

Self-Awareness Scale Directions

Recognition of one's emotions and their effects (emotional awareness), knowledge of one's strengths and limits (self-knowledge), and sureness about one's self-worth and capabilities (self-confidence) are the touchstones of a person's self-awareness. The Self-Awareness Scale can help you identify your own self-awareness by exploring these three areas.

This assessment contains thirty statements. Read each of the statements and decide if the statement is true or false. If it is true, circle the word True next to the statement. If the statement is false, circle the word False next to the statement. Ignore the numbers after the True and False choices. They are for scoring purposes and will be used later. Complete all thirty items before going back to score this scale.

In the following example, the circled False indicates that the item is false for the participant completing the scale:

EMOTIONAL AWARENESS

1. I am able to recognize and acknowledge my feelings   True (1) (False (0)) Score _____

This is not a test and there are no right or wrong answers. Do not spend too much time thinking about your answers. Your initial response will be the most true for you. Be sure to respond to every statement.

(Turn to the next page and begin)

Self-Awareness Scale

EMOTIONAL AWARENESS

1. I am able to recognize and acknowledge my feelings   True (1)   False (0)   Score _____

2. I do not suppress my feelings   True (1)   False (0)   Score _____

3. I understand how my emotions affect other people   True (1)   False (0)   Score _____

4. I can get too emotional   True (0)   False (1)   Score _____

5. My emotions often negatively affect my performance   True (0)   False (1)   Score _____

6. I know which emotions I am feeling   True (1)   False (0)   Score _____

7. I understand the link between my emotions
   and my thinking   True (1)   False (0)   Score _____

8. My emotions often help me to better
   understand situations   True (1)   False (0)   Score _____

9. I cannot change my emotions   True (0)   False (1)   Score _____

10. It is important for me to understand my emotions   True (1)   False (0)   Score _____

TOTAL _____

SELF-KNOWLEDGE

11. I know my limitations   True (1)   False (0)   Score _____

12. I have a good sense of humor   True (1)   False (0)   Score _____

13. I do not like to reflect on what happens in my life   True (0)   False (1)   Score _____

14. I like to be a continuous learner   True (1)   False (0)   Score _____

15. I am open to feedback from others   True (1)   False (0)   Score _____

16. I can describe my strengths   True (1)   False (0)   Score _____

17. I can describe my weaknesses   True (1)   False (0)   Score _____

18. Self-development is not important to me   True (0)   False (1)   Score _____

19. I like to receive different perspectives from
    other people   True (1)   False (0)   Score _____

20. I learn from my experience and do not make
    the same mistakes   True (1)   False (0)   Score _____

TOTAL _____

(Continued on the next page)

(Self-Awareness Scale, continued)

SELF-CONFIDENCE

21. I believe that I am talented   True (1)   False (0)   Score _____

22. Others say I have a great personality   True (1)   False (0)   Score _____

23. I like myself   True (1)   False (0)   Score _____

24. My abilities compare favorably with the
    abilities of others   True (1)   False (0)   Score _____

25. I am easily intimidated   True (0)   False (1)   Score _____

26. I will go out on a limb for what is right   True (1)   False (0)   Score _____

27. I have trouble making decisions under pressure   True (0)   False (1)   Score _____

28. I am very self-confident   True (1)   False (0)   Score _____

29. I will voice views that may be unpopular   True (1)   False (0)   Score _____

30. I will speak out about injustices in the world   True (1)   False (0)   Score _____

TOTAL   _____

Self-Awareness Scale
Scoring Directions

The Self-Awareness Scale is designed to help you to explore your self-awareness.

To score the Self-Awareness Scale total your score for each section and then transfer them to each of the individual scales below.

Emotional Awareness Scale: Total Score from #1 through #10 = _____

Self-Knowledge Scale: Total Score from #11 through #20 = _____

Self-Confidence Scale: Total Score from #21 through #30 = _____

Profile Interpretation

Individual Scale Scores	Result	Indications
Scores from 0 to 3	low	On this scale, you do not score as being very self-aware. It is important for you to do everything you can to better understand your strengths and weaknesses.
Scores from 4 to 7	Moderate	You score somewhat self-aware on this scale. You can benefit from becoming even more self-aware.
Scores from 8 to 10	high	You score self-aware on this scale. Continue to do everything you can to retain your self-awareness.

The higher your score on the Self-Awareness Scale, the more self-aware and emotionally tuned in you are. No matter if you scored in the **Low, Moderate** or **High** range, the exercises and activities that follow are designed to help you learn to increase your self-awareness even more.

Profile Descriptions

EMOTIONAL AWARENESS

People scoring high on this scale are able to quickly and easily recognize the emotions they are feeling and understand the effects that these emotions have on their thinking and actions. They rely on their ability to focus and know the subtle internal signals that tell them what they are feeling. They are able to manage their negative feelings, keep themselves motivated, and accurately tune in to the feelings of those around them. They are able to develop and use good social skills and build long-term, trusting relationships with other people.

SELF-KNOWLEDGE

People scoring high on this scale are able to quickly and easily know and understand both their strengths and weaknesses, work to enhance their weaknesses, work continuously toward greater self-development, and learn from their experiences. They are interested in learning as much as possible about both positive and negative aspects of themselves. They are receptive to open, honest and direct messages from other people, and use these messages to improve themselves. They are aware of their limitations and know where they need to improve.

SELF-CONFIDENCE

People scoring high on this scale are aware of their own capabilities, values, and goals and have the presence and confidence to voice opinions that are different from those of other people. They exude charisma and inspire confidence in people around them. They are able to make tough decisions and follow a course of action they believe in. They believe in their abilities and will work hard to persist through difficulties. They believe in their skills and are able to effectively use the skills they have.

(Continued on the next page)

Emotional Awareness

Becoming aware of your emotions is not something that comes very easily. Part of the reason for this difficulty is that to tune into feelings, you must experience them. When it comes to many negative emotions — sadness, anger, hate and guilt to name a few — they can be very painful to experience. Therefore, most people will tune them out or deny them. By doing so, you spare yourself the agony of feeling bad at the moment, but you prevent yourself from using the valuable information that these feelings can provide you. To get more in touch with your emotions, try some of the following exercises:

Become more aware of the physical behaviors associated with your emotions.

Begin to pay attention to the outward signs of your emotions. Think about a time when you experienced a negative emotion (such as feeling embarrassed when you stood up to speak in front of a crowd). What physical manifestations did you experience (a red face, stomach in knots, feeling faint, etc.)?

What is a time recently when you felt a negative emotion?

_____

_____

_____

_____

_____

What physical manifestations were associated with the emotion?

_____

_____

_____

_____

_____

My Feelings

For the next week, at a particular time each day, write the feelings you experienced during the preceding hours and the cause of those feelings.

DAYS	FEELINGS EXPERIENCED AND CAUSES
Monday	
Tuesday	
Wednesday	
Thursday	
Friday	
Saturday	
Sunday	

(Continued on the next page)

My Feelings *(Continued)*

At the end of the week, review what you have written. Do you find that you experienced certain emotions more than others (anger, optimism, etc.)? What are these emotions?

_____

_____

_____

_____

_____

_____

What caused these emotions? Describe the causes.

_____

_____

_____

_____

_____

_____

What changes could you make to alleviate the negative emotions and experience more positive emotions?

_____

_____

_____

_____

_____

_____

Self-Assessment

Self-assessment is learning as much as you possibly can about yourself and finding out what makes you unique. The following questions are designed to help you with this process:

What are your strengths?

_____

_____

_____

_____

What would others say your strengths are?

_____

_____

_____

What are your weaknesses?

_____

_____

_____

What would others say your weaknesses are?

_____

_____

_____

How do your friends describe you?

_____

_____

_____

(Continued on the next page)

Self-Assessment *(Continued)*

In what ways do you agree with your friends descriptions of you? Explain your reactions.

_____

_____

_____

List two situations when you are most at ease. What do you enjoy about them?

_____

_____

_____

What specific elements are present when you feel this way?

_____

_____

_____

What types of activities did you enjoy doing when you were a child?

_____

_____

_____

What about now?

_____

_____

_____

What motivates you? Why?

_____

_____

_____

(Continued on the next page)

Self-Assessment *(Continued)*

What are your dreams for the future?

_____

_____

What steps are you taking to achieve your dreams?

_____

_____

What do you fear most in your life? Why?

_____

_____

What stresses you?

_____

_____

What is your typical response to stress?

_____

_____

_____

What qualities do you like to see in people? Why?

_____

_____

_____

Do you have many friends with the qualities you just described.

_____

_____

I Am Unique

In the table that follows, identify what makes you unique:

I AM UNIQUE IN THE FOLLOWING ROLES	WAYS I AM UNIQUE
Family	
Work	
Relationships	
Education	
Hobbies	
Other	

Self-Confidence

Self-confidence is the ability to see yourself realistically, capable, able and willing to take on any challenges and master new jobs or skills.

What challenges lie before you that you would like to take on?

_____

_____

_____

What new skills are you confident that you could learn?

_____

_____

_____

What abilities do you possess that you are most confident about?

_____

_____

_____

When you disagree with someone's viewpoint, what do you do?

_____

_____

_____

What types of things would you stand up to other people for?

_____

_____

_____

Things I Can Do Well

To be more self-confident, you need to identify your strengths. In the table that follows, list those things you do well when you are working with your hands, working with ideas and creativity, working with numbers, and working with people.

WHEN I WORK WITH . . .	I CAN . . .
My hands	ex: Repair cars, grow flowers
Ideas and creativity	
Numbers and data	
People	

Things I Cannot Do Well

To be more self-confident, you also need to know your weaknesses and limitations. In the table that follows, list those things you would like to do better when you are working with your hands, working with ideas and creativity, working with numbers, and working with people.

THINGS I WORK WITH . . .	SKILLS I WOULD LIKE TO IMPROVE
My hands	ex: Home repairs, anything mechanical
Ideas and creativity	
Numbers and data	
People	

Self-Awareness

How can being self-aware help reduce your stress?

_____

_____

_____

_____

_____

_____

_____

_____

What have you learned about yourself that surprised you the most?

_____

_____

_____

_____

_____

_____

_____

_____

My Dreams

How will being more self-aware help you reach your life dreams?

_____

_____

_____

_____

_____

_____

_____

_____

_____

How will being more self-aware help you reach your career dreams?

_____

_____

_____

_____

_____

_____

_____

_____

_____

99

Quotations ~ Self-Awareness

"We judge ourselves by what we feel capable of doing, while others judge us by what we have already done."

Henry Wadsworth Longfellow

"Change occurs when one becomes what she is, not when she tries to become what she is not."

Ruth P. Freedman

"You can live a lifetime and, at the end of it, know more about other people than you know about yourself."

Beryl Markham

"Hide not your talents, they for use were made. What's a sundial in the shade?"

Benjamin Franklin

"What is necessary to change a person is to change his/her awareness of himself / herself."

Abraham Maslow

"For a long time, the only time I felt beautiful — in the sense of being complete as a woman, as a human being, and even female — was when I was singing."

Leontyne Price

Quotations ~ Self-Awareness

*"I looked always outside of myself to see what
could make the world give me instead of looking within myself
to see what was there."*

Belle Livingston

*"There is a need to find and sing our own song, to stretch our limbs
and shake them in a dance so wild, that nothing can roost there,
that stirs the yearning for solitary voyage."*

Barbara Lazear Ascher

"To love others, we must first learn to love ourselves."

Anonymous

"I want to do it because I want to do it."

Amelia Earhart

*"I've learned to take time for myself and to treat myself
with a great deal of love and respect ... cause I like me.
I think I'm kind of cool."*

Whoopi Goldberg

Symptoms of Poor Time Management

- Forgetfulness

- Concentration

- Fatigued

- Overwhelmed

- Sleeplessness

- Irritability

- Headaches

- Worry

- Depression

SECTION V:
Personal Change Scale

Name_____

Date_____

Personal Change Scale Directions

Change is constant in the lives of most people today. Change is a part of life that can be very unexpected, sudden, and stressful, if you are not prepared for it. You can learn a set of skills and strategies to effectively deal with and overcome the change that happens in your personal, family, work and financial lives. This scale was designed to help you examine the types of changes occurring in your life that are causing you the most stress, and find ways to take the necessary action to regain control over these change.

The Personal Change Scale contains 32 statements that are related to changes that affect people. Read each of the statements and decide whether or not the statement describes you. If the statement is TRUE, circle the number next to that item under the "True" column. If the statement is FALSE, circle the number next to that item under the "FALSE" column.

In the following example, the circled number under "FALSE" indicates the statement is not true of the person completing the inventory.

I have experienced the following changes in the past year . . .

	TRUE	FALSE
(A) I changed the type of work I do	2	(1)

This is not a test and there are no right or wrong answers. Do not spend too much time thinking about your answers. Your initial response will likely be the most true for you. Be sure to respond to every statement.

(Turn to the next page and begin)

Self-Awareness Scale

I have experienced the following changes in the past year . . .

	TRUE	FALSE
(A) I changed the type of work I do	2	1
(A) My work hours changed	2	1
(A) My work responsibilities increased	2	1
(A) I retired from my job	2	1
(A) I had to learn new technologies at work	2	1
(A) I had trouble with my supervisor	2	1
(A) I had to miss a lot of work	2	1
(A) I experienced a layoff or termination	2	1
(B) I moved my residence	2	1
(B) I married	2	1
(B) I divorced or separated	2	1
(B) A family member experienced a health problem	2	1
(B) My family dynamics changed (birth, adoption, etc.)	2	1
(B) I experienced problems with my in-laws	2	1
(B) I experienced death of a family member or friend	2	1
(B) I have problems with my children's behavior(s)	2	1

(Continued on the next page)

(Personal Change Scale, continued)

I have experienced the following changes in the past year...

	TRUE	FALSE
(C) I changed my place of worship or religious beliefs	2	1
(C) I lost my place to live	2	1
(C) I was not able to take a vacation this year	2	1
(C) I started or finished school	2	1
(C) I experienced a major health problem	2	1
(C) I experienced sexual difficulties	2	1
(C) I made a major change that affected my future	2	1
(C) I developed or lost a close personal relationship	2	1
(D) I was in a car accident	2	1
(D) I experienced legal problems	2	1
(D) I added expensive hobbies or social activities	2	1
(D) I have made a major purchase	2	1
(D) I took on a new mortgage	2	1
(D) I experienced business losses	2	1
(D) I experienced financial losses	2	1
(D) I experienced property loss, damage or theft	2	1

(Go to the Scoring Directions on the next page)

Personal Change Scale
Scoring Directions

This scale is designed to identify those areas in your life in which you have experienced change. To get your scores, total the numbers that you circled for the statements marked (A) in the previous section. You will get a number from 8 to 16. Put that number in the space marked "(A) — Work Life Total" below. Then do the same for the other three scales: (B) — Family Life, (C) — Personal Life, and (D) — Financial Life.

(A) — WORK LIFE TOTAL	=	_____
(B) — FAMILY LIFE TOTAL	=	_____
(C) — PERSONAL LIFE TOTAL	=	_____
(D) — FINANCIAL LIFE TOTAL	=	_____

Profile Interpretation

Individual Scale Scores	Result	Indications
Scores from 14 to 16	high	You are experiencing a great many changes in that aspect of your life. Developing effective personal change management skills would be very important for you.
Scores from 11 to 13	Moderate	You are experiencing some changes in that aspect of your life. You might need to develop some additional personal change management skills to deal effectively with current changes as well as future changes.
Scores from 8 to 10	low	Scores from 8 to 10 on any single scale indicates that you are not currently experiencing a lot of change in your life at this time. Continue to develop effective personal change management skills in anticipation of changes that might occur in your life.

Scale Descriptions

Read the descriptions below and complete the exercises that are included in this scale. No matter how you scored, low, moderate or high, you will benefit from these exercises.

(A) — WORK LIFE — People scoring high on this scale are experiencing stressful changes in their work lives, jobs and careers.

(B) — FAMILY LIFE — People scoring high on this scale are experiencing stressful changes in their family lives.

(C) — PERSONAL LIFE — People scoring high on this scale are experiencing stressful changes in their personal lives.

(D) — FINANCIAL LIFE — People scoring high on this scale are experiencing stressful financial changes.

How Do You Respond to Change?

Change can affect all aspects of your life. Think about the changes you are currently going through. How are these changes affecting you?

How are they affecting your body (headaches, exhaustion, stomach problems, pain, etc.)

_____

_____

How are they affecting your mind (confusion, negative thoughts, forgetfulness, sleep, etc.)

_____

_____

How are they affecting your feelings and emotions (depression, anger, fear, frustration, etc.)

_____

_____

How are they affecting your spirituality (lack of commitment, purpose, meaning in life, etc.)

_____

_____

By learning the signals, you will soon be able to begin taking steps to enhance your transition. When things are changing in your life, you need to learn effective ways to manage yourself. Regardless of what is happening around you in your environment, you will always have control over how you respond to stress, what types of things you do, how you feel, and what you think.

How Can You Cope?

A feeling of control over one's environment is a fundamental need of all human beings. During time of change and transition, unfortunately, it is natural for you to feel out of control. That's when you begin to experience difficulties. You may feel helpless in your situation and unable to change things, or you might even feel like you are a victim and this is happening to only you. Either way, you believe that you are out of control of your own life. You need to start thinking about ways that you can regain control over your situation and your life. To increase your personal power over change in your life, you can do several things:

Take care of yourself

Create a positive inner self

Create a strategy to take action

We will look at all of these strategies individually.

Take Care of Yourself

STAY IN THE PRESENT

Much of the stress that you are experiencing comes from worrying about the changes in your life and how you will work to regain control over these changes. To reduce concerns and ultimately stop worrying, you need to start living in the present moment. When you do this, all of your attention becomes focused on what you are currently doing.

BREATHE

Because breath is vital to life itself, proper breathing is very important and can even be an excellent form of stress reduction related to change in your life. Diaphragmatic breathing, in which you take in long, very deep breaths, is an especially powerful tool for relaxation. In diaphragmatic breathing, you push out your stomach and draw in a long deep breath. Then you exhale as slowly and as long as possible. Repeat this until relaxation occurs.

(Continued on the next page)

(Take Care of Yourself, continued)

EXERCISE

Exercise is another excellent method for combating and managing stress. In our society, the time needed to exercise is often very hard to find, but it is very important that you put aside time each week in order to exercise your body and relieve tension.

FOCUS ON A HEALTHY DIET

Many people admit that during high stress periods they tend to eat more or eat less than usual. They also eat less healthy foods. A healthy diet contributes physically and mentally in a positive way.

RELAX

Progressive relaxation helps you to bring relaxation to all parts of your body through concentrated awareness. It allows you to actually produce relaxation by focusing self-suggestions of warmth and relaxation in specific muscle groups throughout the body.

LISTEN TO MUSIC

Listening to music is probably one of the easiest forms of relaxation. To benefit from the relaxation of music, select music that is soothing and that you find peaceful. To benefit the most from your music relaxation sessions, allow approximately one-half hour of uninterrupted time by yourself daily.

DEVELOP A SUPPORT NETWORK

It is vital to have a supportive network of people who can assist you. Think of your support network as a team of people who can help you through this time of change. By discussing your problems, goals and dreams with people you can trust, you reach out to those people who can help you (and whom you can help if they need it).

For more tools and techniques regarding stress and stress management, please refer to the book:

The Anger & Aggression Workbook, by Liptak and Leutenberg
Published by Whole Person Associates

Create a Positive Inner Self

You now need to learn to draw on your inner resources to increase your personal power over the change occurring in your life. The first thing you must do is to see yourself as capable, resourceful, and a master of change. Complete the following chart to mobilize your strengths.

List strengths from your personal and professional life:

My Strengths

_____

_____

_____

My Skills/Talents

_____

_____

_____

Resources I have Available

_____

_____

_____

Positive Attitudes I possess

_____

_____

_____

What I have to offer

_____

_____

_____

Overcome Self-Defeating Prophecies

Positive inner beliefs and attitudes are important for your success in managing change. When you continue to think pessimistic thoughts, they become self-fulfilling prophesies and you fail to achieve success. Pessimistic thoughts can cause you to feel helpless and hopeless about a change that is occurring in your life. Examples of these types of thoughts:

> "I can't do this."

> "I can't change anything in my life."

> "The future will only get worse."

If you are thinking those types of thought, you need to steer your attitude in a more positive direction. You need to begin using positive affirmations to help guide your thoughts and actions. Positive affirmations are phrases you can use to reprogram your mind to include more positive thoughts. They are brief statements that put you in the proper frame of mind to accept intuitive inputs. Affirmations are a way of sending your brain a message that the desired result has already been achieved. What you state, in the present tense, can easily be achieved. Examples of affirmation that might be used in helping to guide you through change might include:

> "Change is inevitable. I can overcome my resistance to change."

> "Change can be an opportunity for me."

> "Life is changing fast, but I am embracing this change
> and moving beyond my resistance to it."

> "I have control over my life despite recent changes."

> "I am maintaining a positive attitude towards change in my life."

Create Your Own Affirmations

Using the examples of affirmations above, formulate some of your own affirmations below:

_____

_____

_____

_____

_____

_____

To strengthen your coping skills in stressful situations, you need to practice your affirmations on a daily basis. Select one of the affirmations that you feel comfortable with and repeat the affirmation for about five minutes each day for one week.

Regain Control

You need to become more aware of what you have control over and what is not within your control as you work through the change that you are experiencing. The following exercise will help you with this process:

Think about the type of change you are currently experiencing. Describe it.

_____

_____

_____

Describe how the change makes you feel (i.e., scared, angry, happy, etc.)?

_____

_____

_____

Think about and list the things that you can control in this situation.

_____

_____

_____

What types of information do you need to gain about this situation in order to have greater control?

_____

_____

_____

List the things that you cannot control in this situation.

_____

_____

_____

Identify those things you can control, that you would like to focus on immediately.

_____

_____

Create a Strategy to Take Action

TAKE ACTION

People who deal well with change are able to take an active, purposeful approach to change. They look for things that they can change and take action to do so.

From the list of things you identified that you can control (in the last exercise you completed), list those things you can control and how you will take action:

THINGS I CAN CONTROL	HOW I WILL TAKE ACTION

Aspects to Consider

When you experience personal change, you must take stock of the resources you possess and those that you lack. Answer the following questions to identify how well you are handling the changes in your life.

When is it time to make a change, and why or why not?

_____

_____

_____

_____

What change would you like to make?

_____

_____

_____

_____

If this is not the best time, when would be the best time?

_____

_____

_____

_____

How will you know when it is time to change?

_____

_____

_____

_____

(Continued on the next page)

Aspects to Consider *(Continued)*

Can you afford to change? What do you need to consider for this to happen?

_____

_____

_____

_____

Do you feel stagnant? In what parts of your life do you feel like this?

_____

_____

_____

_____

How can you overcome this feeling of stagnation?

_____

_____

_____

_____

What would change look like to you?

_____

_____

_____

_____

How would you be different (both positively and negatively)?

_____

_____

_____

_____

(Continued on the next page)

Aspects to Consider *(Continued)*

Are you taking care of yourself during these times of change? In what ways do you do this?

_____

_____

_____

_____

What do you wish could be different for you during this change?

_____

_____

_____

_____

Describe who you are now?

_____

_____

_____

_____

Who would you be after going through a successful change?

_____

_____

_____

_____

How can this change be viewed as an opportunity?

_____

_____

_____

_____

Change and Others in My Life

How has this change (or will this change) affect other people around you?

PERSON AFFECTED	HOW THEY ARE AFFECTED
My partner	
My children	
My friends	
Other	
Other	

Change in My Life

List what excites you most about change.

_____

_____

_____

_____

_____

_____

_____

_____

_____

List what scares you most about change.

_____

_____

_____

_____

_____

_____

_____

_____

_____

Change Management

What techniques for change management do you like best?

_____

_____

_____

_____

_____

_____

_____

_____

_____

_____

What techniques for change management do you not like? Why

_____

_____

_____

_____

_____

_____

_____

_____

_____

_____

Change Results

Scott & Jaffe* say that there are four results people get based on action they take and control they have:

Mastery – taking action on things you can control helps you feel good and powerful

Ceaseless Striving – Taking action in areas you cannot control leaves you feeling frustrated and angry

Giving Up – Not taking action on things you could control leaves you feeling helpless and hopeless

Letting Go – Not taking action in areas where you have no control leads to relief.

*Scott, C.D., & Jaffe, D.T. (2004). *Managing Personal Change.* Boston, MA: Thomson.

Self-Fulfilling Prophesy Beliefs

Pessimistic beliefs, like the ones below, can leave you feeling helpless and hopeless:

"I can't do this."

"I can't change anything."

"People don't care. Why should I?"

"The future is not within my control."

"People who get ahead are lucky."

"I don't have enough money."

"I'm not good enough."

"My brother gets all of the breaks."

How can you change these beliefs so that they are more positive?

Quotations ~ Change

"You must be the change you wish to see in the world."

Mahatma Gandhi

"Life is change. Growth is optional. Choose wisely."

Karen Kaiser Clark

"We must learn to view change as a natural phenomenon — to anticipate it and plan for it. The future is ours to channel in the direction we want to go . . . we must continually ask ourselves, "What will happen if . . ." Or better still, "How can we make it happen?"

Lisa Taylor

"Things do not change; we change."

Henry David Thoreau

"The one unchangeable certainty is that nothing is certain or unchangeable."

John F. Kennedy

"Change is the watchword of progression. When we tire of well-worn ways, we seek for new. This restless craving in the souls of men spur them to climb, and to seek the mountain view."

Ella Wheeler Wilcox

"Readjusting is a painful process, but most of us need it at one time or another."

Arthur Christopher Benson

"The biggest temptation is to settle for too little."

Thomas Merton

"It's never too late — in fiction or in life — to revise."

Nancy Thayer

wholeperson

Whole Person Associates is the leading publisher of training resources for professionals who empower people to create and maintain healthy lifestyles. Our creative resources will help you work effectively with your clients in the areas of stress management, wellness promotion, mental health and life skills.

Please visit us at our web site: **www.wholeperson.com**. You can check out our entire line of products, place an order, request our print catalog, and sign up for our monthly special notifications.

Whole Person Associates

800-247-6789